10 IDEAS
TO SAVE THE
WORLD
WITH
KINDNESS

Eleonora Fornasari

illustrated by
Clarissa Corradin

Starry
Forest
Books

CONTENTS

THE FIRST STEPS   p. 4

1. BE KIND TO YOURSELF   p. 6

2. USE THE MAGIC WORDS   p. 10

3. KEEP EVERYTHING TIDY   p. 14

4. HELP THOSE IN NEED   p. 18

5. PAY ATTENTION TO OTHERS   p. 22

6. FORGIVE THOSE WHO MADE YOU ANGRY — p. 26

7. TREAT ALL CREATURES WITH KINDNESS — p. 30

8. GIVE UNEXPECTED PRESENTS TO YOUR LOVED ONES — p. 34

9. COMPLIMENT OTHERS — p. 36

10. LEARN TO SHARE — p. 38

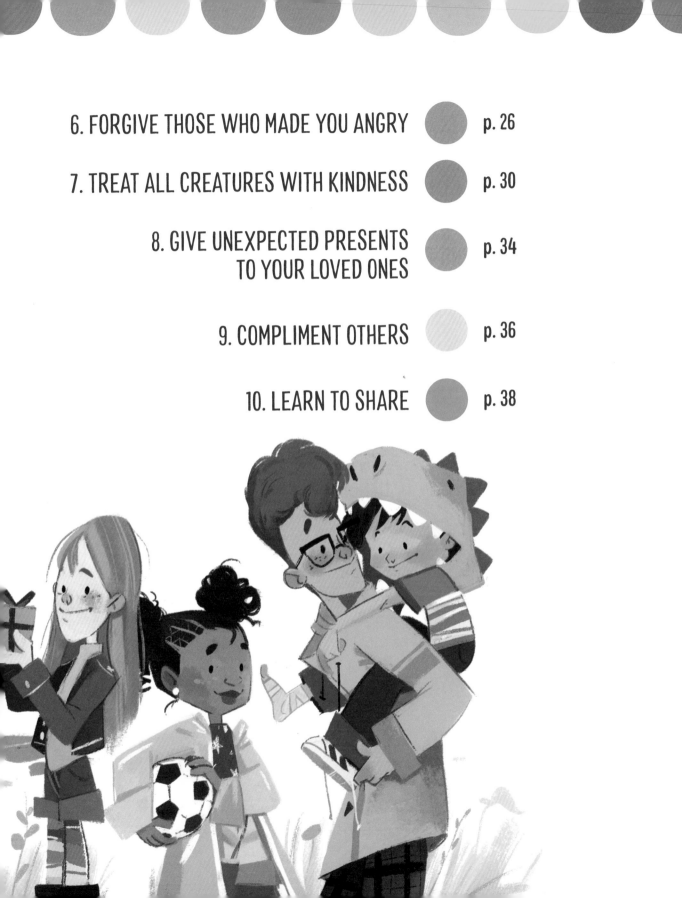

THE FIRST STEPS

Hello and welcome!
This book will help you discover
what it means to be kind.

With the 10 small actions in this book, everybody—even you!—can help make the world a kinder place. Today's fast-paced world is so full of technological advances and opportunities that it might lead us to think we have everything we need. Take a closer look, and you will realize that something is still missing. When we are too busy, we often forget about others. A little more kindness would be good!

Just imagine how wonderful
it would be if we were all more
attentive to others.

Even one small act of kindness can make the world a better place. Just like an ocean that grows drop by drop, we can change the world little by little.

"I always help my brother with his homework," you might say.

Great! That's already an important first step.

There are even more ways to be kind, especially to those you don't know—or get along with—very well.

Everybody benefits from kindness . . . children, adults, and even plants and animals! In order to receive kindness ourselves, we must first learn to give it.

What are you waiting for?

Let's spread kindness! Start by practicing a little (or a lot). You can put these 10 ideas into action, or you can invent your own acts of kindness too. Then, share your ideas—or this book!—with your friends.

TOGETHER, YOU CAN SAVE THE WORLD WITH KINDNESS!

01 BE KIND TO YOURSELF

To be kind, you have to start with the person you know best:

YOU!

Think about it: How many times have you gotten angry at yourself because you weren't good at something? Maybe you didn't win the race at the track meet, or you got the lead role in the school play but forgot your lines onstage.

Remember: Anybody can make a mistake. **It's important not to overreact or blame yourself!** Don't say "I'm a disaster" or "I can't do anything." Do those words sound kind to you?

Instead, look at these setbacks as chances to start again with more enthusiasm.

Turn that frown upside down—a smile will take you miles farther!

If you get a bad grade in school, believe that the next time it will be better. **Then commit to earning a better grade.** Ask your teacher what you did wrong, and study more so you understand the subject better.

If your soccer team loses a match because you didn't score the winning goal, **count to 10**. Getting angry at yourself won't change anything.

Think: If a friend of yours was in the same situation, would you say something mean to them? Of course not! **You would comfort them instead.** You should do the same for yourself. Of course it would be awesome to win first place every time, but that's not always possible! Sometimes you have to accept defeat and be a good sport too.

When you play with your friends, what really matters is being together. Don't you think?

Every time you think something bad about yourself, send it away by magically transforming it into an expression of gratitude.

You could start by **keeping a diary and writing down one happy thought every day**. Thank yourself for being you and for living your life: making new friends, playing games with your family, and learning from a mistake. Mistakes are useful. You could also **write down something that struck you or made your day better**: a poem that you read in school or a stunning landscape that you saw.

There are so many reasons to be thankful every day!

It's a shame to focus only on what we don't have or what doesn't turn out like we planned. **Look at the list of happy thoughts in your diary again.** You will soon realize that there really are a lot of reasons to be kind to yourself.

Another way to be kind to yourself is to set aside some **happy time**. Spend your free time engaging in a hobby, or an activity that makes you happy. Sports are a great option because when you move, the brain produces **endorphins**, molecules that relieve stress. Swimming, dancing, and playing basketball are not only good for being healthy; **they also make you happy**!

If you love painting, **sign up for a painting class**. If you love music, **take some guitar lessons** or ask a friend to teach you. If you love to read, dedicate some time to **reading the latest book or comic from your favorite author**, away from electronic devices and other distractions.

02 USE THE MAGIC WORDS

You don't need a magic wand or a potion to be kind to others—you just need these magic words!

"Hello," "Thank you," "You're welcome," "Please," and "I'm sorry."

They are called magic words because when you say them, they bring happiness and lift your mood as if by magic!

HELLO

When you see someone—a neighbor or your teacher—be the first to greet them in a nice, clear voice! When you greet friends, use a simple "**hello**." Sometimes you can just wave. There are many different greetings, like "good morning" and "good afternoon."

There are even different greetings based on where you are in the world! In **Japan**, people greet each other by bowing; in **Tibet**, people stick out their tongues. But if your friend is not from Tibet, don't use this greeting; they could take your gesture as an insult!

THANK YOU

This simple expression makes everybody happy—the person saying it and the person receiving it! Say "**thank you**" to the waitress who brings your pizza or to the ice-cream man who hands you your cone. Sometimes others are so happy to help someone kind and polite, they'll do something nice in return. (Maybe the ice-cream man will give you an extra scoop!) **Kindness attracts kindness.**

YOU'RE WELCOME

If you receive a wholehearted "thank you," remember to respond with "**you're welcome.**" It's a beautiful expression because it indicates that you have done something good for someone. If your classmate thanks you because you lent them your pencil or your grandfather thanks you for the drawing you made, be kind too: "you're welcome" is the phrase you need.

PLEASE

If you have a request or you need to ask someone for help, remember to say "**please**." Do you want your dad to help you pump up your bicycle tires? Are you hoping that your grandma will make you your favorite cake?

Ask politely: when you are kind to others, they will be happy to listen and give you a hand.

I'M SORRY

This is the most difficult to say! Saying that you're sorry means admitting that you were wrong, and nobody likes doing that. It requires a lot of courage, but it's worth it. If you played with a ball in the house and broke your mom's favorite vase, or told a mean joke about your brother, you should know exactly what to say: "**I'm sorry**."

You will see that every bad feeling disappears as if by magic!

THERE ARE TIMES WHEN WORDS ARE NOT NEEDED.

If your mom comes home tired from work, and it looks like she feels down, welcome her with a big smile: it will lighten the mood! If you know a classmate who is always sad and grumpy, give them a smile as a sign of friendship and encouragement. **Who knows, they might smile back at you sooner or later!**

Smiling is contagious!

Don't believe it? Try this: smile at every person you come across on the street or on your way to school.

Want to bet how many people will smile back? Scientists call this "emotional contagion." When we smile, our body sends a signal to the brain to be happy. So, the more you smile, the better you and everyone around will feel!

Truly magic, huh?

03 KEEP EVERYTHING TIDY

Kindness means thinking of others, and there's no better way to do that than showing respect toward the spaces—and people—around you!

Cleaning up shows everyone that you care!

When you get up in the morning, **make your bed**. Plump up the pillow, pull the sheets up, and lay the blanket or comforter on top. It doesn't matter if there are creases in your blanket or your pillows aren't propped up right; you are giving your room a clean and well-kept appearance **in your own way**! Also remember that your room has many other things to be kept tidy.

Each object has its own place, right?

Books on the shelves or in your schoolbag, clean clothes in the drawers or in the closet, dirty clothes in the laundry basket! And toys? You might have bins or containers for them. If not, ask an adult.

That's not all!

The rest of the house needs tidying up too.
Let's clean!

Step one: Put on some music! Ask an adult to help, and you will see that it is more fun to tidy up while singing along!

● Clean the house with your family. It's fun to help the people you love!

One way to do this is to help **clear the table**: put plates, glasses, and utensils in the sink (be careful about knife edges!). Fold the tablecloth and put it away with the napkins.

And what about shoes that are left everywhere? Put them neatly inside a shoe cupboard to avoid tripping over them!

Apart from your house, it is important to keep communal spaces—such as roads, parks, and schools—tidy and clean.

Many people visit these places, so there will be a lot to do—and a lot of people who will appreciate your work! **Even your small daily actions can make a huge difference.**

 If you walk your dog, always pick up its poop with a bag. You'll keep the sidewalk clean, and you'll do the next passersby a favor!

 When you and your friends have picnics in the park, put all empty bottles in the recycling and put garbage in the trash bins.

The park will stay clean, and you will avoid stepping on litter!

Wherever you are, do your part and clean up paper, cardboard, or garbage that ends up on the floor or ground.

You can show your respect for others by also respecting shared spaces! Shared spaces should be treated as if they were your own.

Would you like it if someone scribbled all over your schoolbag with markers? Of course not! **Drawing on school desks or park benches is never a good idea.** You can express your creativity by drawing on paper, singing, or playing music.

A great way to express your feelings creatively is making a gift for someone.

If you want to let your friends know how much you care about them, you can make them a nice bracelet. You just need a few colorful threads, beads, shells, or any other material you like and, of course, your imagination!

04 HELP THOSE IN NEED

People need help!

But if you're distracted—maybe with your head buried in a video game—you won't notice those who need help.

The next time you head to school, the supermarket, or the park, keep your eyes peeled. You might see an elderly person struggling to carry their bags or a pregnant woman who needs to sit down.

Be the first to be kind!

Offer to give them a hand by carrying their heavy bags or by giving up your seat on the bus or the subway. Give them a smile too!

When you are more attentive, you will see many more opportunities to be kind every day.

What matters is making the move!

Strangers are not the only ones who need help.

Perhaps someone in your family is having a hard time. If your sister has a cold, let her watch her favorite TV show, even if you don't really like it. If your grandpa struggles to read, offer to read his newspaper out loud to him. If your mom or dad comes home tired from work, help them set the table and prepare dinner. How many times do they do things for you? **This is the perfect chance to return the favor and be kind, without being asked.** Every now and then, grown-ups need help from kids too.

If your friend struggles with certain subjects in school, **offer to help with homework**. With your help, they'll understand their mistakes and learn how to study more efficiently.

It's too easy to only help the people we love.

It's important to still help the bully from next door, the classmate you always fight with, or someone who has very different opinions from yours. Everyone needs kindness: adults and children, nice people and not-so-nice people. You must give kindness to receive kindness.

One small, kind action after another can change the world.

Remember: the ocean is formed one drop at a time.

Did you know that there is a World Kindness Day?

It is celebrated on **November 13** every year. The Japanese celebrated it for the first time in Tokyo, in 1988. It spread around the globe soon after! On this day, everyone is challenged to do at least one kind action.

Similarly, in Italy, they celebrate **Suspended Coffee Day**. Based on an ancient Neapolitan tradition, this day is the epitome of "pay it forward." When someone walks into a cafe, they order a "suspended" espresso. Then they pay for two espressos and receive one. The second coffee is then saved for someone who can't afford it.

Do you like the idea? Share it with your friends as a way to celebrate **World Kindness Day**. It could be an occasion to challenge one another to see who can make the kindest gesture!

 Here's one way to do this: make a die with cardboard and write a kind action on each face, then roll it and see what side faces up. Then start spreading kindness all around!

05 PAY ATTENTION TO OTHERS

Kindness is about helping others, but it is also about paying attention to them.

What does that mean? It means playing with the girl at school that everybody ignores as if she were invisible. We all need to be "seen." Kindness is the ability to see others and understand what they feel, even if they don't speak it out loud. Not everybody has that courage, so it's up to you to realize that and make the first step. Sometimes a nice word, a smile, some advice, or sincere listening is enough.

Pay attention to people when they're talking to you. If you get a text message while you're hanging out with a friend, look at your phone later! And try not to interrupt or finish other people's sentences. Wait for people to finish speaking before you do.

Get into the habit of asking others how they are. You know, sometimes adults tend to reply, "I'm fine" instinctively, but that's not always the truth. They do that partly out of politeness and partly because they are not used to showing that they are struggling. They will appreciate the attention; they will feel understood and may tell you what worries them. And if you have an older neighbor who is always alone, stop by to chat with them one day. Someone might just be waiting for you to ask them how they're feeling!

Kindness is simple, although sometimes it seems difficult.

You may not have the will, time, or patience. **According to scientists, being selfless is good for those who receive kindness and those who offer it.**

Empathy, the ability to share and understand others' feelings, is at the core of every kind gesture. Imagine putting yourself in someone else's shoes; this helps you understand what troubles them. Interestingly, human beings are not the only creatures that can empathize with others. Many social animals, like elephants and rats, empathize and selflessly care for others. Chimpanzees, for instance, help each other find food and regularly groom each other.

According to a Japanese study, most rats decide to help a friend in trouble, even if that means giving up on food. Who would have thought that? Rodents, it turns out, are kind!

At the United Nations headquarters in New York, there is a mosaic titled *Golden Rule*. It shows men, women, and children from different cultures and religions around the world. Underneath the mosaic, there is a quote:

"Do unto others as you would have them do unto you."

The artist Norman Rockwell created the mosaic to portray empathy. When you put yourself in other people's shoes, then you will be able to treat them the way you would like to be treated.

Do you know that **the Golden Rule is present in many religions and philosophies** around the world?

For example, the philosophers **Confucius** and **Plato** theorized and shared this philosophy many centuries ago. But Confucius lived in China, and Plato lived in Greece—very far apart! The Golden Rule is also common in many West African and Indigenous cultures. Today, it is applied in several contexts. From school to politics, it has become a way of life for many. Do you like it?

FORGIVE THOSE WHO MADE YOU ANGRY

If everyone were to do one kind act a day, the world could become a better place! But there are times when not everyone sees eye to eye. Arguments make it easy to forget about kindness.

When you are angry at a friend, do you pout or ignore them? If your friend apologizes, don't make them feel guilty about their mistake.

People can be wrong sometimes (even you), and the words "**I'm sorry**" are magical because they leave everything in the past and let you start anew . . . not with a new argument, but a new page, where you are closer friends than ever! Being kind means leaving misunderstandings behind and moving on.

Of course it's not easy, but nobody ever said that kindness was easy. Work up your courage, and face the challenge!

It's important not to lash out at someone, even if they don't apologize. We can't change the behavior of others—but we can work on our own! So if a friend doesn't apologize . . .

Why not make the first step and break the ice?

Try this: approach your friend and ask them to play with you, as if nothing had happened before. Like magic, both of you will soon forget the reason why you argued in the first place. You will find new energy to spend even more time together.

Remember the Golden Rule:

If you were the one in the wrong, wouldn't you want to be forgiven too?

So don't hesitate! Start by setting a good example.

Maybe you are the one who made someone angry, even if you didn't mean to.

Let's say your dad asked you to stop playing and to do your homework. Instead of listening, you decided to ignore him and kept playing with your toys. Later, your dad yelled at you for not following his instructions, and you felt hurt about being scolded. Don't take it personally; instead, think about it from your dad's point of view. Most importantly, let your anger go.

And don't forget the magic words! Add a simple, sincere **"I'm sorry**." It doesn't take much to straighten out a day that started off in a bad way.

Remember: it is not worth it to stay angry.

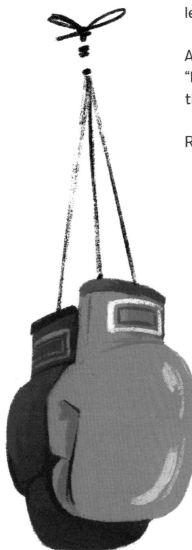

A big smile is much better than a frown, don't you think?

Did you know that scientists have proven that forgiveness is good for the heart?

It requires a bit of practice . . . but we can learn forgiveness just like we learn to swim or to run. The more you forgive people, the easier it becomes!

Forgiveness makes you happier.

When you're angry, you waste time dwelling on it and getting upset. Forgiveness makes you feel lighter and relieves your mind of negative thoughts. **Why stay angry when you can forgive and be happy?**

Think about it—
only you have the answer.

07 TREAT ALL CREATURES WITH KINDNESS

Did you know that even plants deserve kindness? Just like our human friends, if we take care of plants, they will grow strong and healthy. If we mistreat them, they will suffer. They are living creatures with sensitivity and intelligence too.

Perhaps it is not necessary to use all the magic words with them, but talking to them or playing them some music could help them feel a little less lonely. Yes, you heard correctly! **According to some studies, plants even have their own taste in music.**

Interesting, huh? Music is essential in humans' lives too; it helps us relax and unwind. This seems to happen with plants as well. What a fun way to train your green thumb!

Like other living creatures, plants are not all the same, and each one of them needs specific care. Some need watering every day and love the sun; others need very little water to survive and prefer the shade. If you are not sure about what your plants need, ask a parent or guardian for advice.

Remember that pulling leaves and picking flowers for no reason is damaging. Plants are crucial for the survival of our planet. Have you heard of **photosynthesis**? This is the process through which plants receive nutrients and, at the same time, produce oxygen that is then released into the air.

Plants are very kind:

They allow us to breathe! Another great reason to treat them well.

What about our animal friends?

They are very sensitive to kindness too. Whether it's a cat, a horse, or a swan, they all deserve our attention and our respect. **Like plants, animals are not toys: if you decide to get a dog, you need to be ready to look after it for the rest of its life!** Animals need a lot of things, just like human beings: food, rest, play, care (especially if they fall ill), comfortable spaces, and most importantly . . . love! So before asking your parents to get a pet as a present for your birthday, be sure that you can make the time to look after it. If you can, find a reliable breeder, or even better, visit your local **animal shelter** or contact an **organization that rescues animals** and adopt your new best friend.

How to show kindness to your pet:

- Take your pet to the vet regularly and make sure that it has all the required vaccinations.
- Keep your pet's space clean. Change your cat's litter box every day.
- Research the best food for its breed and feed your pet regularly.
- Play with your pet, but only when it wants to; sometimes even animals want to be left alone.
- If your pet needs a lot of exercise, take it for a walk regularly, or supervise as needed. Dogs tend to need walks the most, but cats need playtime and hamsters need to burn off energy sometimes too!
- Be patient with your pet if it makes a mistake. Don't yell at it or (even worse) kick it!
- Always cuddle your pet gently.

If you think that someone is mistreating an animal, tell an adult and report the abuse to animal control.

This is another way to care for animals. Can you think of more ways?

08 GIVE UNEXPECTED PRESENTS TO YOUR LOVED ONES

A present is a thoughtful way to show your love for someone on their birthday or a special occasion. **What if there isn't a special occasion?** Surprise someone with a gift anyway!

Think about someone you would like to give a present to.

You don't need to buy expensive gifts. Often the best presents are the ones that come from the heart. **Get ready to unleash your imagination!**

If your grandpa has a green thumb, give him a potted plant to care for. Draw a portrait of your mom that she can put in her office, which will make her think about you all day. Or bake your dad his favorite cake with your older siblings. Just knowing that you thought of them—and made them homemade gifts—will make them happy! **What other creative gifts can you think to make?**

What matters is if your friend likes the gift— not if you do!

If your friend is crazy about a certain actor or actress, it doesn't matter if you don't like him or her, a poster would be a perfect present! Another exciting gift could be something that holds great value to you, even if it has been used. Gift someone your favorite book, and share your passion with a friend!

It will not only be an act of kindness, but also a token of friendship!

Even a thoughtful card or letter will be appreciated; they warm the heart and prompt a big smile. You could write one for a neighbor that accepted a delivery while you weren't home or for a friend you haven't seen in a while.

If you think about it, there are so many reasons to give people a small present!

09 COMPLIMENT OTHERS

Like the magic words, you can give compliments to express kindness out loud!

Compliments must always be sincere and come from the heart. If your mom is good at dancing, why don't you tell her? She will be happy to hear it. When your dad prepares your favorite pizza, remember to show him your appreciation. He will be happy that you like it, and perhaps he will make it for you again soon! And what about your grandparents, who are so loving and protective of you? Don't miss the chance to let them know you value them whenever you have the opportunity.

Remember: A compliment is almost always appreciated by the receiver. **Everyone needs to feel accepted and appreciated for who they are and what they do**, but not everyone gets to hear it. The next time you have a chance, tell someone what you like about them without hesitation.

It is important to recognize your friends' strengths too.

Which friend makes you laugh the most? Who is the fastest runner or the best artist? When you come up with an answer, be sure to tell them! Surprise your friends with the compliment game, and challenge each other to come up with the best compliments at unexpected moments. Wait until you see how happy it makes them—and you!

Remember:
Everyone has
good qualities you
can compliment . . .
Even you!

Instead of expecting compliments from others, start by complimenting yourself.

Take the time to think of what you are good at. Are you good at giving advice? At baking cookies with your mom? At completing complex puzzles? Write it on a sheet of paper, and read it every now and then.

10 LEARN TO SHARE

Today, the word "share" has taken on a different meaning, thanks to social media. We share posts, videos, images, and news on the web. We post them online, and someone reads or watches them. The verb "to share" comes from the Old English word "scearu," which originally referred to the split in a tree trunk and evolved to mean **a part of something that can be divided between people**. Think about how many things can be divided with someone else, as an act of kindness and generosity. If your classmate has forgotten their lunch at home, offer them some of yours. **This way, you can eat in each other's company.**

Or **share a comic** with your friends; you read it first, then pass it on to others. So once everybody has read it, you can all take turns to impersonate the characters in the story. Isn't that a great idea?

Or **share your favorite joke** with your family and friends. It's more fun to laugh with others, right?

Share good news too! When you get an exciting present, tell your friends. Even adults share good news with the people they love. If your parents or guardians decide to buy a big house with a yard or receive a job promotion, they'll probably tell you and their parents and friends too. **When you share with others, you will all be happy together.**

It is said that "happiness is true only if shared!" When you share something with someone, or you show selflessness, your brain releases **dopamine** and **serotonin**, which some call the "**happiness hormones.**"

Do you want to be happy? Then be kind!

What are you waiting for? Start practicing the 10 kind gestures in this book. And if you see that they are not enough, come up with more: **kindness has no limits!**

ELEONORA FORNASARI

Eleonora lives in a nice house surrounded by trees and squirrels . . . and full of books! From a young age, she filled notebooks and diaries with lots of stories and imaginary characters. Today she is an accomplished author and TV writer. She teaches at the Catholic University of the Sacred Heart in Milan, Italy.

CLARISSA CORRADIN

Clarissa was born in Ivrea, Italy, in 1992. She attended the Albertina Academy of Fine Arts in Turin, where she studied painting and illustration. Now she passionately illustrates children's books, including White Star Kids' *Avery Everywhere* series.

White Star Kids® is a registered trademark property of White Star s.r.l.
© 2020 White Star s.r.l.
Piazzale Luigi Cadorna, 6
20123 Milan, Italy
www.whitestar.it

Starry Forest® is a registered trademark of Starry Forest Books, Inc.
This 2021 edition published by Starry Forest Books, Inc.
P.O. Box 1797, 217 East 70th Street, New York, NY 10021

ISBN 978-1-951784-05-8

Manufactured in Romania

2 4 6 8 10 9 7 5 3 1

03/21